The Olden Time Series - Volume I

HENRY MASON BROOKS

1886

TABLE OF CONTENTS

INTRODUCTION.

While this work does not pretend to be a history, it will yet present many historical facts. Its object is to show from old newspapers, which are not accessible to all, such items and comments upon a variety of subjects as might be supposed to amuse or instruct both old and young.

It is not the easy thing that many imagine to examine, read, and select from a vast number of newspapers such matter as is believed to be worth reproducing. Possibly to some it would seem to be a stupid and an uninteresting work. The Compiler, however, has found it a source of pleasure to make and arrange these selections; and the value of his work will be greatly enhanced if these volumes should prove of interest to any considerable number of persons.

There appears to be from year to year a growing taste among the most cultivated people for quaint and curious reminiscences of the Olden Time; and as these volumes will be of a handy size for the pocket or carpetbag, it is hoped that they will be welcomed by many who would not undertake to read a more pretentious or cumbersome work on similar topics.

Salem, Mass.,

April, 1885.

CURIOSITIES OF THE OLD LOTTERY

People of the present generation who look over files of old newspapers are filled with astonishment to see the great number of lotteries which are advertised, for many years, down to as late a period as the year 1826. The Faneuil Hall Lottery, the Harvard College Lottery, the Rhode Island College Lottery, the Massachusetts State Lottery, and lotteries for a bridge over the River Parker, for Marblehead, for the Williamstown Free-school, for Episcopal and Congregational Churches, were all advertised, with numerous other projects. A lottery was proposed for the purpose of finishing Bunker Hill Monument, although the scheme was not carried out. It is perhaps not generally remembered that this monument was at length completed by means furnished by a Ladies' Fair, in 1840, and handsome contributions by several individuals. Among other contributors was the celebrated danseuse Fanny Ellsler, who was at that time giving performances in Boston. Some of the best men in the community were interested in recommending the various schemes, and members of churches, men in high repute, bought and sold the tickets. In Salem, Mass., such well-known and esteemed citizens as John Jenks, Daniel Jenks, Thomas C. Cushing, of the "Gazette," John Dabney, the postmaster, Colonel John Russell, and the now venerable and respected Edward H. Payson—who, at the age of eighty, is still cashier of the First National (formerly the Commercial) Bank, to which office he was elected in 1826—sold tickets; so did Colonel John Hathorne. Colonel Henry Whipple, who is remembered as one of our best citizens, kept, in connection with his bookstore, a "Fortunate Lottery Office." Other names might be mentioned, but we think we have given enough to show the respectability of the calling. The better the man, the better the agent. Indeed, it was generally thought to be just as respectable to sell lottery-tickets as to sell Bibles; and we have seen them classed together in the same advertisement. Our observations have been confined chiefly to Boston and

Salem prints, but we have no doubt that similar matter could be found in other papers. We propose now to give liberal extracts from some of the old advertisements of the different schemes, which will, we think, confirm what we have already said on the subject. Let us take first from the "Boston Gazette" of May 19, 1760, the lottery to raise $1,000 towards building a bridge over the River Parker, in Newbury. The managers were the first men in the place, and the tickets were sold by men of excellent standing in Boston.

Bridge

NEWBURY, May 17, 1760.

SCHEME OF A LOTTERY

FOR raising a Sum of Money for the building and maintaining a Bridge over the River Parker, in the Town of Newbury, at the Place called Old Town Ferry (in pursuance of an Act of the General Court, passed in April 1760) Wherein Daniel Farnham, Caleb Cushing, Joseph Gerrish, William Atkins, Esq., and Mr. Patrick Tracy, Merchant, (or any Three of them) are appointed Managers. The acting Managers are sworn to the faithful Performance of their Trust.

Newbury-Lottery Number Four, consists of

5000 Tickets, at Two Dollars each; 1655 of which are Benefit Tickets of the following Value.

1 of 500 Dollars, is 500 Dollars.
4 of 100 are 400
5 of 50 are 250
6 of 40 are 240
10 of 30 are 300
14 of 20 are 280
45 of 10 are 450
75 of 8 are 600
1495 of 4 are 5980

—— ——

1655 Prizes, amounting to — 9000 Dollars.
3345 Blanks.

——

5000 Tickets, at Two Dollars each 10 000
To be paid in Prizes, 9000

——

1000 Dollars.

Remains to be applied for the Purpose aforesaid.

Two Blanks only to one PRIZE.

THE Bridge aforesaid is already built, and upon a Settlement of the Accounts, and Demands relative thereto, the Managers of the former Lottery for that Purpose, were found to be greatly in Debt: The Charges of building the Bridge, and prosecuting the Lottery, amounting to much more than what was allowed to be raised by the former Act of the General Court—therefore the present Lottery is allowed.

AND since the said Bridge so well answers the Expectation of the Public, and the Travelling that Way thereby is rendered much more easy and pleasant; the Managers doubt not there will be a great Demand of the Tickets, from a Principle of encouraging and promoting a Work of such general Utility, if there were no other Inducement. But when they consider how much this Scheme is calculated in Favour of the Adventurers, there being many Prizes of great Value, and but two Blanks to a Prize; they doubt not of a very speedy Sale of the Tickets.

Tickets purchas'd at Boston, if fortunate, will be paid off there. Public Notice will be given of the Time and Place of Drawing; and as soon as finished, the Prizes will be published in the Boston Gazette and Country Journal. Gold as well as Silver will be received for Tickets; and the Prizes paid off accordingly. Prizes not demanded in Twelve Months after Drawing, will be considered as given to the common Stock for building and maintaining the said Bridge, and will be so applied.

Tickets are to be Sold by the Managers in Newbury, by Ebenezer Storer, Esq., and Son; Mr. Timothy Newell; William and James Jackson, and the Printers hereof in Boston.

The town of Taunton, Mass., was favored by a lottery grant in 1761 to aid in clearing the Great River.

Taunton, March 16. 1761.

PUBLICK NOTICE is hereby given to all Persons who are so disposed to encourage the Clearing of Taunton Great-River, (so beneficial to the Trade of this Province) by adventuring in the LOTTERY granted for that Purpose, That the Managers of said Lottery have determined to begin to draw the First Class on Tuesday the 27th Day of April next; the Town of Taunton having voted to take off all the Tickets that shall remain unsold at that Day;—And all Persons who have taken Tickets to dispose of, are desired to return them, or the Money for them, by the First Day of said April.

☞ Tickets are yet to be had of Messir's Gould and Company, and of Green and Russell, Printers in Queen Street, Boston.—As also of the Managers at their respective Dwellings in Taunton.

Next we will take from the "Boston Post Boy" of November, 1762, the scheme to raise money to rebuild Faneuil Hall, after the fire of 1761. It will be noticed how small an amount was reserved for the purpose for which the Lottery was granted,—only $1,200. It seems as if a very small sum subscribed by every freeholder would have produced more money. If the population of Boston at that time was, say, twenty thousand, or three thousand families, fifty cents for every head of a family would have raised a larger sum than could possibly have been raised by the expensive and questionable process resorted to. At first sight it may seem strange to us that this was not thought of at the time; but when we reflect that even in our enlightened times people are quite as thoughtless about the processes of raising money for charitable or public purposes,—witness the numerous fairs and raffles which are constantly taking place,—we are not so much amazed at these old financial operations, nor do we think we can boast much of our superior morality when we look around and see how some things are managed nowadays.

BOSTON, November 1, 1762.

SCHEME OF A LOTTERY

For Raising a Sum of Money for Re-building Faneuil Hall; agreeable to an Act of the General Court, wherein Messieurs Thomas Cushing, Samuel Hewes, John Scollay, Benjamin Austin, Samuel Sewall, Samuel Phillips Savage, and Ezekiel Lewis, or any Three of them, are appointed Managers, who are Sworn to the faithful Discharge of their Trust.

Faneuil-Hall Lottery, No. One, Consists of 6000 Tickets, at Two Dollars each, 1486 of which are Benefit Tickets of the following Value, viz.

Dollars.

1 Prize of 1000 Dollars, is 1000
1 of 500 is 500
2 of 200 are 400
12 of 100 are 1200
20 of 50 are 1000
20 of 20 are 400
30 of 10 are 300
200 of 6 are 1200
1200 of 4 are 4800

——— ———

1486 Prizes, 10800 Dollars.
4514 Blanks.

———

6000 Tickets at 2 Dollars each, is 12,000 Dollars.
To be paid in Prizes, 10,800

———

Remains 1200 Dollars,
to be applied to the Purpose aforesaid.
The Necessity of a large and convenient Hall in such a Town as this, upon

all Public Occasions, can't be disputed. The Rebuilding Faneuil-Hall has therefore been generally approved of; and the Encouragement it will meet with from the Public, will, we doubt not, be in some Measure proportionable to its Importance: We promise ourselves therefore a speedy Sale of the Tickets; and hope we shall soon be able to draw.

Public Notice will be given of the Time and Place of Drawing; and as soon as the Drawing is finished, a List of the Prizes will be published in Edes and Gill's Boston Gazette, andc. and the Money paid to the Possessors of the Benefit Tickets, in Twenty Days. Gold as well as Silver will be received for the Tickets, and the Prizes paid off in like Manner.

Prizes not demanded within Twelve Months after Drawing, will be deem'd as generously given for the Purpose aforesaid, and will be applied accordingly.

☞ Tickets may be had of the Managers, or of Green and Russell, in Queen-street, who will receive Prize Tickets in Land-Bank LOTTERY.

In 1782 the State of Massachusetts granted a lottery for the benefit of the paper-mill at Milton.

The Clergy were often asked to use their influence to promote special schemes. For instance, the Leicester Academy at Lancaster, Mass., wishing to raise about $800, advertised on June 28, 1790, a lottery, the scheme comprising three thousand tickets at $2.00; and the managers, Edmund Heard and Ephraim Carter, say, "As the design of this Lottery is for promoting Piety, Virtue, and such of the liberal Arts and Sciences as may qualify the Youth to become useful Members of Society, the Managers wish for and expect the aid of the Gentlemen Trustees of the Academy, the Reverend Clergy, and all persons who have a taste for encouraging said Seminary of Learning." Comment on this is unnecessary. As unscrupulous persons often sold drawn tickets,—for it seems there were irregularities even in those days,—the following advertisement warrants the tickets undrawn,—

Wheels very rich!

A FEW undrawn Tickets in Amoskeag Lottery for sale by John Russell.

☞ The highest prize being so fixed as to come out whenever Chance shall direct it, it stands purchasers in hand to be seasonable in their applications. July 24, 1807.

Lottery Price Current.—In Boston, Amoskeag Tickets, warranted undrawn, 6 dolls. In Salem, at Russell's 5.50—at Cushing and Appleton's, not warranted, 5.

Further Information.—The Amoskeag highest prize, of Eight Thousand Dollars, is still undrawn, and the wheels are extraordinarily rich, having gained, since the drawing began, upwards of Six Thousand Dollars. There is therefore every probability that the scrip will soon rise. Those who intend to purchase for the sake of a chance for the highest prize, are advised to do it before it is drawn out of the wheel, which may be to-morrow. Those who purchase for the sake of a cheap ticket, would do well to wait till afterwards. July 24, 1807.

*** If any body wants

TEN THOUSAND DOLLARS,

they are requested to call on

JOHN RUSSELL,

who will, for a trifling consideration, put them in a

way to realize that, or another sum of less

magnitude, in the course of September

next, when the rich Wheels of Hatfield

Bridge Lottery will begin

to move.

Tickets will rise on the first of September to 5.50—Prize Tickets exchanged.   (1807)

In 1776 the Continental Congress endeavored to raise a large sum by means of a lottery. On the first of November of that year the following Resolve was passed,—"That a sum of money be raised by way of lottery, to be drawn at Philadelphia." A committee was then empowered to manage this lottery, and agents were appointed in the several States to sell the tickets. From causes difficult now to explain, the drawing, which was to have taken place in 1777, was postponed from time to time, until finally, it is said, the whole scheme proved a failure. Many of the adventurers being large losers, much bad feeling was produced towards the Government. The design was to raise the money in the way of a loan. There were four classes of tickets, a hundred thousand in each,—$10, $20, $30, and $40; in all $10,000,000. In Lossing's "Field-Book of the Revolution," from which we derive this account, may be seen a copy of one of these lottery tickets. Probably the people were too poor at that time to furnish the requisite sum of money, and so the tickets did not sell readily; or the lottery may have been badly managed.

Congregational Churches used to raise money by lottery, as appears by the following advertisement in the "Columbian Centinel," May 5, 1792,—

NEWPORT LOTTERY TICKETS

A few TICKETS, in the Newport Congregational Church Lottery, which commences drawing the 10th instant, may be had at No. 61 Long-Wharf if applied for immediately. May 5.

At a town meeting held in Salem, Mass., on Dec. 28, 1789, "George Williams, Esq., General Fisk, and Joseph Sprague, Esq., were chosen a Committee to estimate the expense of clearing out the Channels in the North and South rivers; and to prefer a petition to the General Court for the grant of a Lottery to aid the town in so beneficial an undertaking." We believe this project was never carried through; but we are of opinion that some residents of Salem would now welcome even a raffle, if in that way their North River could be purified, as at present no other method seems so likely to succeed, judging from the controversy which has been going on in that city for several years without effecting any result.

The "Massachusetts Centinel," May 22, 1790, notifies the "Friends of Science" that "a few ... Williamstown Free-school Lottery Tickets ... may be had of the Printer."

MARBLEHEAD, APRIL 3. The highest Prize in the State Lottery was drawn by a number of Females: About thirty were joint possessors of that fortunate number and five others: The highest share in them did not exceed one dollar, and the lowest was nine pence, expressive of the different abilities of the concerned; by which circumstance, the property of the prize is most agreeably divided: It has excited a smile in the cheek of poverty, nor diminished the pleasure of those in easy circumstances.

Massachusetts Gazette, 1786.

Providence Street-Lottery.

CLASS 3d.

THE Managers present the public with the following SCHEME of a

LOTTERY, granted by the Hon. General Assembly of this State, at their January Session, A.D. 1795, for raising a Sum of Money to defray the Expences of Finishing, in a durable Manner, a Street at the North End of this Town.

This being the great Continental Thoroughfare and Post Road, and much frequented at all Seasons by Persons on Foot and Horse-Back, and by Teams and Carriages, merits the greatest Attention to its Improvement from Town and Country.

The old Road was crooked and inconvenient, the new Street is Streight, and secured in such a Manner as to be passed in Carriages at all Times with Ease and Safety.

The Utility and Necessity of this work, so obvious to every one, and the great Chance to Adventurers, there being only about Two Blanks to a Prize, induce the Managers to rely on the Patronage of the Public, for a rapid Sale of the Tickets.

5340 Tickets, at TWO DOLLARS each, are 10,680 Dollars, to be paid in the following Prizes, subject to no Deduction.

Dolls. Dolls.
1 Prize of 1000 is 1000
1 300 300
1 200 200
4 100 are 400
10 50 500
20 30 600
40 20 800
50 10 500
100 6 600
1482 3 4446

——— ———

1709 Prizes, 9346
3631 Blanks, 1334

——— ———

5340 Tickets, at 2 Dolls. each, is 10680
To commence drawing the 1st June next.

TICKETS may be had by applying to the subscribers; and the Prizes paid on demand. Prizes not demanded within six months after the drawing, will be considered as generously given for the finishing the work.

EBENEZER MACOMBER, } Managers.
SAMUEL THURBER, jun.
STEPHEN RANDAL,
BENJ. TURPIN,

TICKETS in the above Lottery, may be had of Eben. Larkin, of Wm. P. Blake, and at the Post-Office, Boston,   Feb. 21, 1795.

Those who remember the late Colonel John Russell, at one time president of the Bank of General Interest in Salem, and a kindly, benevolent "gentleman of the old school," will read with interest his advertisement of "A New Dispensary," from the "Salem Gazette," March 24, 1807.

A New Dispensary!

NUMEROUS are the instances that can be cited of a less, a much less, sum than Twenty Thousand Dollars having restored to their pristine vigor precarious circumstances, and of making the poor become rich! Let stubborn prejudices be laid aside, and an immediate resort made to that Grand Antipoverty Corrective, CASH, which is now proffered as a sovereign remedy for all the complaints that poverty is heir to:—in asserting the superior efficacy of this preventive of the evils attendant on a state of poverty, it is not intended to trespass on truth—let it be fairly tried, when the 'majesty of its own worth' will be manifest. The door is now open for the reception of such as would like to try the experiment:—There is Hatfield Bridge Lottery, which commences drawing the 15th of next month; this affords a potion of Eight Thousand Dollars; if, after a fair trial here, the desired effect is not produced, then there is the Harvard College Lottery, which commences in May, which has the highly balsamic cordial of TWENTY THOUSAND DOLLARS, which will produce the most wonderful effects, by giving a solid tone to the regions of the pocket, and by enriching and invigorating the whole system, as can be satisfactorily tested:—Twenty Thousand Dollars would

"Cheer the heart, and make the spirits flow!"

Perseverance is highly recommended, and if the wishes are not gratified by the attainment of the desired object, the consoling reflection will recur, that—"there are not quite two blanks to a prize"—which is more than can be said of quackery in general. Tickets and Quarters for sale by

John Russell.

To-Morrow the price of Tickets rise—purchasers can be accommodated until 9 o'clock, this evening.

A handsome Premium given for Essex County Money.

The Boston "Herald of Freedom," in December, 1789, advocates a lottery for that town for the benefit of the poor, among other things, and to supply the town with lamps to light occasionally for the "safety of the citizens," etc.

A citizen would wish to know why among the many lotteries now in being, there is not one for the benefit of this town? Can it be said we have no need of any?—Sure there are many uses the net proceeds of a lottery may be converted to, for this town's benefit: Though he means not to dictate, yet would suggest the following;—that a granary might thereby be opened, and the poor supplied with different kinds of grain, at a reduced price;— that several parts of the town might be paved; which would serve to employ many of the industrious poor among us;—and that the town might be supplied with Lamps, which by being occasionally lighted would tend to the safety of the citizens. From these, among other beneficial effects, he hopes the town will have a meeting, and petition the General Assembly at their approaching session for leave to establish a lottery for the above, and other, useful purposes.

From the "Salem Gazette," May 10, 1791.

No. 17221, which drew 2000 dollars in the Semi-annual State lottery, was paid on Friday last, by Messrs. Leach and Fosdick, in Boston. The proprietors were four Africans belonging to Newport.

From the "Columbian Centinel," June 5, 1790.

Two apprentices belonging to Mr. Bemis, Paper-Maker, in Watertown drew the 1000 dollar prize in Williamstown Lottery.

Advertisement

Columbian Centinel, April 28, 1790.

Lines on the prizes drawn by the poor widows of Marblehead. From the "Columbian Centinel," April 24, 1790.

CASTALIAN FOUNT

FOR THE CENTINEL.
LINES,
On the Prize of FIFTEEN HUNDRED DOLLARS being drawn by the poor Widows of Marblehead, written there.

WHENCE this increase of wealth? What bounteous hand
Grants more than sanguine Hope could e'en demand?
Nor Chance nor Fortune shall the merit claim,
Those fancied forms to Folly owe their name:
Such airy phantoms ill deserve our lays;
A nobler object calls forth all our praise.
That Pow'r Supreme, who knows no great or small,
But looks unchang'd with equal eye on all—
Who lifts the poor from their unnoted state,
And humbles at his will th' aspiring great—
Whose hand divine hath held us in its span,
And fed, and cloth'd us since our lives began—
Hath, sure, this last rich gift in kindness sent,
To be improv'd, and not in riot spent;
A further proof of Heav'n's indulgent care,
In which our poorer neighbours ought to share.
Accept, Great God, what thankful hearts can give,
For life and health, and all the means to live!
Much thou hast added to our former store;
O keep us still as humble as before!
What thou hast lent, direct us how to use,
And teach us when to give, and when refuse.
To others freely let our bounty flow,

But not beyond Discretion's limits go.
Then let us live as useful as we can—
Grateful to God—beneficent to man—
Possess obscure the bliss of doing good,
Never so well explain'd as understood.
Fortune
20,000!! 5,000!! 1000!!! Dollars.
WHO is there that would not give 6 dols. 50 for one of the above sums, or 1 dollar 75 cts. for a quarter of one of them. Chances to gain one are now selling at the above prices, at KIDDER and CO's, Lottery, Insurance on Tickets, and Intelligence Office, No. 9, Market-square.
Tickets and Quarters will be insured during the drawing of the Lottery, which presents an excellent chance for saving the cost of Tickets!! Adventurers will do well to call!!!
Boston Palladium, June 9, 1807.
LUCK INDEED!!
YESTERDAY No. 2159 in the Kennebec Bridge Lottery, came up the valuable Prize of
ONE THOUSAND DOLLARS!!
and as usual was sold, at the most fortunate and truly lucky Office of
RALPH HUNTINGTON,
No. 14, Exchange-street, 3 doors from State-street. This is the 5th Capital Prize in the Kennebec Lottery, sold by RALPH HUNTINGTON.
The highest Prize of $25,000 will be drawn this afternoon, at 3 o'clock. R.H. has for sale, a few shares in a Company of 100 Tickets, and a few Quarters. Jan. 19.
Boston Palladium, 1819.
No. 4072, the most fortunate number, in the State Lottery, sold at the Printing-Office, in Salem, we hear is the property of upwards of a dozen poor widows belonging to Marblehead.
Columbian Centinel, April 10, 1790.
Anglers
FORTUNE'S ANGLERS:
A NEW LOTTERY SONG.
TUNE—"There are sweepers in high life as well as in low."
In the fish pond of fortune men angle always,
Some angle for titles, some angle for praise,
Some angle for favor, some angle for wives,
And some angle for nought all the days of their lives:
Ye who'd angle for Wealth, and would Fortunes obtain,
Get your hooks baited by Kidder, Gilbert and Dean.
Some angle for pleasure, some angle for pain,
Some angle for trifles, some angle for gain,

Some angle for glory, some angle for strife,
Some angle to make themselves happy for life:
Ye who'd angle, andc.
Some angle for wit, and some angle for fame,
Some angle for nonsense, and some e'en for shame,
Some angle for horses, some angle for hounds,
For angling's infinite, it never new bounds:
Ye who'd angle, andc.
G. and D. and W. and T.K. for the accommodation of those who purchase Tickets of them, keep Daily Lists of Prizes and Blanks, and a complete statement of the wheels, which can be examined at the close of each day's drawing, free of expense. And for the convenience of their country-customers publish in every paper, while any lottery is drawing, the numbers of all prizes over seven dollars, state of the lottery, andc. andc.

Persons at a distance may be assured, that the most punctual and strict attention will be given their orders for tickets, (post paid) enclosing cash or prize tickets, addressed to Gilbert and Dean, 79, State street, or W. and T. Kidder, 9, Market-square, and the earliest information sent them respecting the fate of their numbers.

*** Prize Tickets in all the Lotteries taken in pay for other tickets.   March 24

Boston Repertory, March 24, 1809.

Washington's Birth Day.

IT is a little remarkable, that the great

UNION CANAL LOTTERY

commences drawing on the 22d inst. being the birthday of Washington—
and the first drawn blank will be entitled to
FOUR THOUSAND DOLLARS!
Boston Palladium, 1819.

PATRIOTISM OF THE LADIES

The Ladies of Massachusetts have ever been distinguished for their patriotism; and although their peculiar province is to soften the cares, and soothe the sorrows of life, yet they have never neglected any proper and decent opportunity of advancing the publick good:—When the Ladies found that Government had established a Lottery to ease the taxes of the people, they generally became adventurers, and it is pleasing to find that this their Patriotism has been in some measure rewarded, by their sex sharing the FIRST CAPITAL PRIZE.

Columbian Centinel, April 28, 1790.

CONNECTICUT MANUFACTORY

LOTTERY,

For raising the Sum of three Thousand two Hundred Pounds.

The Managers being under oath, and having given bond for the faithful discharge of their trust, present the Public with the following

SCHEME.

1 Prize of 5,000 Dollars, is 5,000

1 - 2,500 - - 2,500

1 - 1,500 - - 1,500

5 - 1,000 - - 5,000

10 - 500 - - 5,000

15 - 200 - - 3,000

50 - 100 - - 5,000

100 - 50 - - 5,000

300 - 25 - - 7,500

325 - 15 - - 4,875

500 - 10 - - 5,000

4,400 - 8 - - 35,200

1 last drawn Blank, - - 760

_____ _____

5,709 Prizes, 85,335
11,358 Blanks.

_____ _____

17,067 Tickets at 5 Dollars each, is 85,335
Not two Blanks to a Prize.
Subject to a Deduction of 12 and an half per Cent.
This Lottery was granted by the honorable General Assembly for the encouragement of a Manufactory of Woolen, Worsted, and Cotton, in this State, under the superintendance of William M'Intosh, (late of London) a Gentleman of Information and Experience in the construction and use of the new invented Machines for that Purpose, a Number of which being completed he hath now in use.
The Managers flatter themselves that all Persons will become Adventurers in this Lottery, who consider the importance of the Object for which it was granted, as they will thereby aid one of the most valuable Manufactories attempted in this State, since the era of Independence.
They contemplate a speedy sale of the Tickets, and engage a punctual payment of the Prizes, if demanded in six Months after drawing, which is to commence on the 21st day of October next, and when finished, the fortunate numbers will be published in the Connecticut Journal.
TIMOTHY JONES, } Managers.
HENRY DAGGETT,
ELIAS BEERS,
WILLIAM LYON,
NATHAN BEERS,
New-Haven, May 16, 1794.
Tickets to be had of the Managers, and of Thomas Hilldrup, at the Post Office Hartford.
Connecticut Courant, Hartford.
The General Assembly of Rhode Island grant a lottery for the "advancement of religion" in 1794. Advertised in Boston.
SCHEME of a
LOTTERY—
Granted by the Honourable General Assembly of the State of Rhode-Island, andc. at their Session held in October, 1794, for the purpose of finishing a House for Public Worship—Consisting of 3000 Tickets, at 3 dollars each, to be paid in the following Prizes, subject to a Deduction of Twelve and an Half per Cent.
1 Prize of 1000 Dollars, is 1000
1 500 500
2 Prizes of 250 500

5 100 500
10 50 500
20 25 500
50 10 500
1000 5 5000
——— ———
1089 Prizes. 9000
1911 Blanks.
———
3000 Tickets.

As this Lottery was granted for promoting Public Worship, and the advancement of Religion, we flatter ourselves that every well-wisher to Society and good Order will become cheerful adventurers. For those who adventure from Motives of Gain, the Scheme is advantageously calculated, there being less than two Blanks to one Prize—and Bonds given for the faithful performance of the trust reposed in us.

As a considerable number of the Tickets are already engaged, we expect to draw said Lottery by the first of May next. Prizes not demanded within six months after drawing will be deemed as generously given towards finishing said House. The time and place of drawing will be notified—a List of the Prizes will be immediately published in the Herald of the United States— and paid on demand.

MARTIN LUTHER, } Managers.
WILLIAM BARTON,
DANIEL KELLEY;
Warren, Nov. 28, 1794.

Tickets and Quarters of Tickets in the above Lottery, may be had at the Post-Office, Boston.

Jan. 31, 1795.

GOOD FORTUNE IN THE LOTTERY REALIZED.

Boston, May 12, 1791.

ON Monday last, Messrs. Edward Esty and Oliver Johnson, of Westmoreland in the State of New-hampshire, produced the ticket No. 6052, which drew the highest prize (TEN THOUSAND DOLLARS) in the Semi-annual Lottery, to Mr. JOHN KNEELAND, (the Manager who signed that number, and whose tickets have been remarkable for drawing the highest prizes) who gave them a check on the Bank for their money, which they received the next day.

A circumstance relating to the purchase of this ticket may be worth relating. The owners of it were at Charlestown, late on the Saturday evening preceding the drawing of the lottery, and had mounted their horses to go on their way home, before they recollected wanting a ticket. Mr. Bridge

(who sold tickets in Charlestown) happened to be then up, at his house—
and went to his store, in the dark, and from his desk took the fortunate
number, and sold it to the above fortunate persons.

Salem Gazette, May 17, 1791.

Dartmouth College scheme, as advertised in the "Salem Gazette" in 1796.

Dartmouth College Lottery.

CLASS SECOND.

THE Managers of Dartmouth College Lottery present to the Public the
following Scheme of the Second Class, in which they have aimed to meet
their wishes by making a larger proportion of valuable prizes than usual;
they flatter themselves that the same Public Spirit will be displayed, by
encouraging the sale of Tickets in this, that was so fully manifested in the
former Class.

SCHEME.

Prizes Dolls. Dolls.

1 of 3000 is 3000
1 1000 1000
4 500 are 2000
10 200 2000
20 100 2000
30 50 1500
80 20 1600
100 10 1000
1650 6 9900

——— ———

1896 Prizes. 24,000.
4140 Blanks.

———

6000 Tickets, at 4 Dollars each, are 24,000.

Subject to a deduction of twelve and an half per cent.

Of the above prizes of 500 Dollars, one of them will be placed to the first
drawn blank, and the other three to the three last drawn blanks.

This Class will positively commence drawing at Concord, on the 1st day of
December next; and when completed, a list of Prizes will be immediately
published, and the prizes paid on demand.

JONATHAN FREEMAN, } Managers.
BENJAMIN CONNOR,
WILLIAM J. KENT,

Concord, Aug. 17, 1796.

TICKETS sold by JOHN JENKS and CUSHING and CARLTON.

Harvard College appears to have seen the "misery of adventurers drawing
blanks which were worth nothing," and remedied the matter in 1811,
according to the following advertisement from the "Salem Gazette."

Look on this!

THE serious evil which has fallen upon a great many adventurers, by purchasing Tickets in former lotteries, and drawing blanks which were worth nothing; appears now to be remedied.—The managers of the Fifth Class of Harvard College Lottery, have in their wisdom taken the misery of this evil into consideration and have given us a scheme preferable to any former one; by which it seems that from 20,000 to 50,000 dollars will be distributed among persons whose tickets are drawn blanks in this lottery, which commences drawing in a few days; and the greater part of the Tickets are now sold. Whole and Quarter Tickets for sale at the Bookstore and Lottery Office of

HENRY WHIPPLE,

June 7, 1811.   No. 6, Wakefield Place.

A Boston paper of 1811 has the following:

Washington Monument Lottery

WILL commence drawing in Baltimore the 4th day of September next.

The Capital Prizes are

1 of 50,000 dollars,

1 of 30,000,

1 of 20,000,

2 of 10,000,

3 of 5,000,

20 of 100 Tickets,

And many of 2000, 1000, 500, andc. andc.

Tickets and Quarters for Sale by Simpson and Caldwell, of Baltimore, who request all persons who wish to purchase Tickets and Quarters in the above Lottery, to forward their orders, post paid, enclosing cash, to Messrs. BRIDGE and RENOUF, No. 79, state street, Boston; and they may depend on their orders being promptly executed.

Price of Tickets 11 dollars—Quarters 2 87.

Aug. 13, 1811.

The "Union Canal Lottery" was got up in 1814 to benefit Boston and "make it advance like New York." Here is a notice of the scheme from a Salem paper,—

Union Canal Lottery.

First Class.—Twenty-Five Thousand Dollars.

It rarely happens that the object of a Lottery is interesting to the whole community. To save the Metropolis of New-England from declining in its commerce and consequence on the return of a general peace—to open its internal resources, to unite New-Hampshire and Vermont to Massachusetts, by bonds of mutual benefit, as permanent as the rivers and canals, by which their intercourse will be carried on—to make Boston advance like New York, supported by a populous, extensive and productive back country, are considerations into which every reflecting man, every merchant, and every owner of real estate, must enter and must feel. It is therefore, confidently expected, that a Lottery, granted to complete the great undertaking of opening Inland Navigation, will receive peculiar support; and that many who have not been in the habit of adventuring in Lotteries, will be willing and desirous of contributing to the success of this for the sake of its object.

The Highest Prize will be paid in ninety days after the drawing shall be completed; and all other Prizes in sixty days, and payment will be made in bills generally current in Boston. Prizes must be demanded in one year from the end of the drawing of the Class.

This Class will commence drawing in Boston, on the 12th December next.

Tickets to be returned on or before the 2d December.

BENJAMIN WELD,

WILLIAM A. KENT,

ANDREW SIGOURNEY,

Boston, Nov. 8, 1814.   Managers.

After lotteries had been drawn, notices frequently appeared in the papers announcing the names of the lucky prize-winners. For instance, a Boston paper of 1790 says: "The highest Prize (£3,000) in the New York Lottery was drawn by 2 deserving Servant girls of New York;" and in Sept. 21, 1793: "The highest prize in the 4th Class of the State Lottery ($1,000) was drawn by Mr. Benjamin Blodgett, of this town;" and the "Salem Gazette" of 1815 says: "Luther Martin, Esq., has drawn $15,000, the Highest prize in the Baltimore Hospital Lottery;" and it adds: "Those who envy the good Fortune of Mr. Martin will call on Cushing and Appleton for Tickets in the Harvard College Lottery." In November, 1790, the "Salem Gazette" says that the call for tickets in the Massachusetts Semi-annual Lottery "has been so great in the other States that the Managers expect to draw much sooner than the time which was at first mentioned;" also that the tickets in the Marblehead Lottery are meeting with a rapid sale; and concludes that "this does not indicate a scarcity of Cash."

Here are some curious advertisements:—

From the "Columbian Centinel," Boston, May 22, 1790.

Williamstown FREE SCHOOL Lottery.

We are authorised to assure the Publick, and we do assure them—that the 7th Class of this Lottery will not only commence drawing on Monday next, but will positively be completed on Tuesday morning—and a list of Prizes will be published in the Centinel the same week.

The metropolis of Massachusetts hath ever been celebrated for the attention it hath paid to the education of its youth. In the elder world, a Franklin hath been a living testimony of it, as well as in the younger. But not confined to the youth of the town is this benevolent disposition—it

extends to the remotest parts of the Commonwealth; and hath been abundantly manifested in the liberal encouragement given to the Williamstown Free-School Lottery. The Class to be drawn on Monday next, will perhaps, be the last opportunity our citizens may have to gratify their humane wishes—which they will not let pass unimproved, especially as great pecuniary profit may attend the gratification.
"Salem Gazette," Nov. 24, 1812.

GALVANISM

It has been found by Dr. Nauche, at Paris, that a person perfectly blind may be made to see very lively and numerous flashes of light, by bringing one extremity of the voltaic pile into communication with the hand or foot, and the other with the face, skin of the head, or even the neck. In like manner, a person in the gloom of poverty may be made to perceive very lively and numerous flashes (say 20,000) of good fortune by bringing one extremity of a ragged bank bill into communication with the Book-Store and the other with the Lottery-Office, one door west of Central Building.
N.B.—Two grand piles are now offered to the public—Harvard College, where the process is now in active operation, and Plymouth Beach which is in a state of preparation.
"Salem Gazette."
Writing
Taught in One Lesson!!
PERSONS of any age, sex, or capacity, let their Chirography be never so bad, may by one exercise make a very good hand of it. The means are found in the Scheme of Harvard College Lottery, which contains a most superb assortment of capital prizes. Persons desirous of securing the advantage of this dispatchful tuition will apply (wholes $5, quarters 1.38) to Cushing and Appleton, at their Lottery Office and Bookstore, one door west of Central Building.
1811.
From "Salem Gazette."
"WHO WANTS A GUINEA?"
THIS Comedy by Coleman, has for some years past, been often read and justly admired; the name now appears to have lost its novelty.
Something of greater magnitude is wished for; something which will furnish

the possessor with more than a competency; which will assist the industrious and enterprizing man, in accomplishing his laudable wishes.

This surely must be the true Philosopher's Stone, which wise men of all ages have sought for in vain.—This inestimable Gem, with some of the virtues usually ascribed to it—will, after the Fifth Class of Harvard College Lottery has completed drawing, belong to some person or persons who will now generously lend a hand to patronise this excellent institution.

Those who are disposed from motives of interest or actuated by a wish to promote and encourage literature; will please call for Whole or Quarter Tickets, at the Book-Store and Lottery Office of

HENRY WHIPPLE,

May 17, 1711.   No. 6, Wakefield Place.

"Salem Gazette."

Surprising Gain!

IT is true as strange, and strange as true, that the wheels of Harvard College Lottery have actually gained, in the few revolutions they have made, no less than

5157 Dollars!

Now is the tide, which, taken at the flood, leads on to fortune, as the immortal Shakespeare would say. The undrawn tickets have all the advantage of this gain, in addition to the common chance at the outset. A few for sale (wholes 6 dolls. quarters 1.63) at Cushing and Appleton's superlatively lucky Lottery and Exchange office, and federal book shop, one door west of Central Building, Essex street.

In 1808 there was a "Real and truly Fortunate Lottery Office" at No. 1 Summer Street, Boston, and Detroit Bank bills were taken in payment for tickets.

Truly fortunate

Real and truly Fortunate

LOTTERY OFFICE, No. 1 Summer street, opposite the North west corner of the New State House—

D. BEMAN'S list of Capital Prizes, sold by him at his Real and truly Fortunate Lottery Office—as follows,

No. 9031, a Prize of 8000 Dolls.

14459 a Prize of 1000 do.

8638 a Prize of 500 do.

8950 a Prize of 500 do.

39 a Prize of 500 do.

3988 a Prize of 500 do.

12722 a Prize of 200 do.

Besides a great number of 100—50—20, and 7 Dollar Prizes—amounting to a handsome Fortune—over the whole cost of all the Tickets ever sold at his office.... This is to be considered the Real and Truly Fortunate Lottery

Office.

Tickets, Quarters and Eighths in the 4th Class of Harvard College, which is now drawing—10,000 Dollars highest prize. A complete list of all the Drawing may be seen days and evenings, gratis.

Prize Tickets and Detroit Bank Bills taken in payment; such as are guaranteed are taken at par. and those of another kind at a discount.

June 3.   (5w)

The highest prize in the Providence Episcopal Church Lottery was $8,000, and the drawing was to begin on Sept. 29, 1800. Tickets were sold in Boston at E. and S. Larkin's, 47 Cornhill. Gilbert and Dean, 56 State Street, Boston, make the following exhibit of the Golden Shower in 1803.

It is impossible to tell on whom the GOLDEN SHOWER will fall!

Golden shower

YE that have the least relish to obtain 8000 dollars for a trifling sum, be "up and doing!" The third class of Hadley Lottery, will commence drawing the 15th of June.

Remark.—The object of this Lottery is of great public utility—that of improving South Hadley Canal, in order to make it permanent and beneficial to the public—and the Proprietors, in this arduous undertaking, have to cut through an entire mass of rocks for three miles! Laudable and praise-worthy perseverance!

Tickets for sale by GILBERT and DEAN, Magazine and Lottery Office, No. 56, State-Street, where a correct list of all the prizes and blanks will be exhibited, during the drawing.

May 25, 1803.

In the "Salem Gazette" will be found the advertisements of two of the College Lotteries. Rhode Island College is now Brown University.

R. Island College Lottery.

THE Corporation of the College, wishing to discharge in the best manner the trusts reposed in them for the education of youth, and finding their funds inadequate to this purpose, have obtained of the General Assembly of the state of Rhode-Island and Providence Plantations the grant of a Lottery. As the sole object of this is the public good, it is hoped that the exertions of the Corporation will meet the wishes and secure the co-operation of all the friends of science and virtue. The College was founded entirely by the generosity of individuals. Though it has received no patronage from the legislative body, yet through the assiduous labours of its officers it has become considerably distinguished, and, it is hoped, has merited the attention of the public. It, however, is under great disadvantages for want of larger pecuniary resources. Of the necessity of these for the establishment of a complete system of liberal education, every one must be sensible who entertains a just conception of the vast extent of science.—Those who are disposed to promote the Lottery now brought forward, may be assured that the whole business will be transacted with the utmost exactitude and fidelity. Of this they cannot doubt, when they are informed that the management of it is wholly under the direction of the following respectable Committee, appointed by the Corporation, viz. John Brown, Esq. Welcome Arnold, Esq. Mr. John Mason, Col. William Russell, and Mr. John P. Ives.

The Subscribers, being appointed by the Committee as Managers of the Lottery, and having given bonds according to law, now offer to the public the following

SCHEME

CLASS FIRST.
dols. dols.
1 Prize of 4000 is 4000
1 2000 2000
2 1000 are 2000
4 500 2000
20 100 2000
40 50 2000
60 30 1800
100 20 2000
1000 12 12000
3000 9 27000

_____ _____

3328 Prizes, amounting to 46000
Drawback, 8000

_____

9000 Tickets, at 6 dollars each, are 54000
The drawing of this Lottery will commence on MONDAY, the 16th day of APRIL next, and continue till it shall be completed. A list of Prizes will be published in the Providence Gazette, and the Prizes paid on demand. Those not called for within six months after the drawing of the Lottery, will be considered as generously given to the College.
JOHN WHIPPLE,
SAMUEL THURBER, jun.
Providence, November 17, 1797.
TICKETS in the above Lottery to be sold at this Office, and at John Dutch's Auction Room, Essex-Street.

Harvard College Lottery.
CLASS FIRST,
Not two Blanks to a Prize.
TWENTY-FIVE THOUSAND TICKETS, at 5 Dollars each, are 125,000 Dollars, to be paid in the following Prizes, subject to a Deduction, of twelve and an half per Cent. for the purposes of the Lottery.

Prizes Dols. Dols.
1 of 10,000 is 10,000
2 5,000 10,000
3 2,000 6,000
6 1,000 6,000
10 500 5,000
20 200 4,000
60 100 6,000
90 50 4,500
100 40 4,000
120 30 3,600
161 20 3,220
200 10 2,000
7,585 8 60,680

8,358 Prizes, 125,000
16,642 Blanks.

25,000

THE above Class will positively commence drawing in the Representatives' Chamber, in Boston, on THURSDAY, 13th November next, and will continue from day to day, and be completed with all possible dispatch. A list of Prizes will be immediately published, and the Prizes paid on demand.

The Managers believe it enough, to induce the Public to become Adventurers, to inform them, that the object of this Lottery is to erect a new Building, at the University in Cambridge, for the further accommodation of the Students. The Friends of literature are to be found every where, and when its cause can be served, and a good chance for personal emolument at the same time presents itself; this double inducement, it is conceived, must operate in favor of the Lottery.

The Managers of this Lottery, had the conducting of the late State Lottery—the Public will do them the justice to say, that the strictest punctuality as to the time fixed for Drawing, and in the payment of Prizes, was observed by them in that Lottery—they pledge themselves for the same punctuality in this.

BENJAMIN AUSTIN, jun. } Managers.
GEORGE R. MINOT,

SAMUEL COOPER,
HENRY WARREN,
JOHN KNEELAND,
Boston, July 14, 1794.
TICKETS are sold by J. JENKS, D. JENKS, J. HATHORNE, J. DABNEY, and W. CARLTON, Salem.
Major Benjamin Russell, in the "Boston Columbian Centinel," March 26, 1791, says:
The National and State Legislatures being in recess, there is a "plentiful scarcity" of domestick occurrences, at this time.—This is locally remedied by the Lottery, which seems to arrest the attention of all ranks of citizens.—To describe the symptoms of the disease is impossible—all are fascinated—all expect to be the favoured children of Fortune.—The rich court her smiles, as eagerly as the poor—and whilst, O! fickle Goddess, the Young pour forth their supplications for thy favours,
"With falt'ring pace, and feeble knee,
See Age advance, in shameless haste;
The palsied hand is stretch'd to thee,
For Wealth, it wants the pow'r to taste."
The delusion is general—and general must the mortification be. But as attention must be paid to the infatuation—we have endeavoured, by a regular publication of the fortunate numbers, to alleviate its frenzy.
On March 29, 1814, Messrs. Bridge and Renouf, the well-known brokers, of 79 State Street, Boston, gave notice that a prize of $500—No. 3,394—"had" been "drawn in the Plymouth Beach Lottery." This number had been "sold by them to several young Gentlemen who purchased 30 Tickets;" and they also announced that the drawing was "suspended until the next Tuesday, when the first drawn ticket will be the highest prize, Twenty thousand Dollars;" and besides this, that "there are remaining to be drawn four prizes of $1,000 each, and four prizes of $500 each."
It should be noticed that there was, even in its most flourishing days, a difference of opinion among individuals in regard to the morality of the lottery, as men must differ on all subjects; so that it is perhaps only fair to cite a specimen or two of the communications which appeared in the papers in reference thereto. A writer in the "Salem Gazette," June 29, 1790, says:—
OF LOTTERIES.
Lotteries have of late been a very productive source of revenue in this State.—The moral tendency of them has been supposed by some to be injurious to society; and government have been careful to grant them for such purposes only, as that the probable benefit should outweigh the evil. By this means we have seen the interests of literature supported—the arts encouraged—the wastes of war repaired—inundations prevented—the

burthen of taxes lessened, andc. Manufactures might also in this way be established. Those which will not support themselves, it is true, will not benefit the community; but there are very important ones, which in their infancy require the nursing hand of government—to such the produce of lotteries might be beneficially applied. There exists a spirit of adventure in all societies, which will lead a number to throw themselves into the hands of Chance in one way or another, and which, under the direction of a wise Legislature, may be made to subserve their best interests. The monies raised by lotteries cannot impoverish the community—as they are not sent abroad, but only taken out of one pocket and put into another.

There is also in the same paper, of Feb. 25, 1794, another communication, in which the writer apparently takes an entirely opposite view, and quotes a letter of Joel Barlow to the National Convention of France, in which will be found some rather strong language. When one considers the place where these views appear to have been adopted, and recollects the horrible scenes of the French Revolution, which were even then being enacted, one wonders whether the French authorities valued human life as much as they did property.

ON PUBLIC LOTTERIES

MR. CUSHING,

AS our Legislature have lately had under consideration a bill, for granting a Lottery to Harvard College, I beg you will publish what our countryman, Mr. Barlow, said on the subject of Public Lotteries, in his Letter to the National Convention of France. It is as follows:

"SINCE I am treating of morals, the great object of all political instructions, I cannot avoid bestowing some remarks on the subject of Public Lotteries. It is a shocking disgrace of modern governments, that they are driven to this pitiful piece of knavery, to draw money from the people. But no circumstance of this kind is so extraordinary as that this policy should be continued in France, since the revolution; and that a state lottery should still be reckoned among the permanent sources of revenue. It has its origin in deception; and depends for its support, on raising and disappointing the hopes of individuals—on perpetually agitating the mind with unreasonable desires of gain—on clouding the understanding with superstitious ideas of chance, destiny and fate—on diverting the attention from regular industry, and promoting a universal spirit of gambling, which carries all sorts of vices into all classes of people. Whatever way we look into human affairs, we shall ever find that the bad organization of society is the cause of more disorders than could possibly arise from the natural temper of the heart. And what shall we say of a government that avowedly steps forward, with the insolence of an open enemy, and creates a new vice, for the sake of loading it with a tax? What right has such a government to punish our follies? And who can look without disgust on the impious figure it makes, in holding the scourge in one hand, and the temptation in the other? You cannot hesitate to declare, in your constitution, THAT ALL LOTTERIES SHALL BE FOREVER ABOLISHED."

In November last, the Convention, in conformity with the foregoing sentiments, passed the following decree:

"Lotteries, of whatever nature they may be, or under whatever denomination they may exist, are suppressed."

In 1791 the Massachusetts Legislature granted to the proprietors of the Cotton Manufactory in Beverly four hundred tickets in the lottery about to be drawn, and three hundred in the next Semi-annual State Lottery. "Some people, out-doors," says the "Salem Gazette," March 8, 1791, "murmur at this as an ill-judged act of liberality; but perhaps they are not acquainted with the arguments which induced the grant. The disposition of Government to foster our infant manufactures is certainly laudable." This is unquestionably good reasoning; for, granted the premises that lotteries are ever beneficial, then there was no reason why aid should not in this way be extended to business enterprises which were to give employment to the people, as well as to schools and colleges. Employment must be provided as well as education. The Beverly Cotton Manufactory, Stone, in his History of Beverly, claims to be the first manufactory of its kind established in America, that at Pawtucket having been the second; and he also states that it was visited by General Washington on his tour through the country in 1789. The leading proprietors in this enterprise were George and Andrew Cabot, Israel Thorndike and Henry Higginson, men of the highest reputation in New England for integrity and honor.

From the "Salem Gazette," Dec. 25, 1812:

The Historical Dictionary,

By Ezra Sampson, author of the Beauties of the Bible, is one of the most useful little works of this nature which we have seen. It contains much in a small compass. Its subjects are Natural and Civil History, Geography, Zoology, Botany and Mineralogy, arranged in alphabetical order, and explained in such a neat and intelligible manner, as to render it worthy of being (according to its design) a Companion for Youth. We select the following article as a specimen of the work.

LOTTERY,

A kind of public game at hazard, in order to raise money for the service of the state. A lottery consists of several numbers of blanks and prizes, which are drawn out of wheels, one of which contains the numbers of the tickets, and the other the corresponding blanks and prizes. Besides the consideration that this, as well as all other kinds of gambling for money, tends to corrupt the public morals, it is also to be considered that the purchasers of the tickets are never permitted to play the game on fair and equal ground. The world neither ever saw, nor ever will see, a perfectly fair lottery; or one in which the whole gain compensated the whole loss; because the undertaker could make nothing by it. In lotteries the tickets are really not worth the price which is paid by the original purchasers, and yet they often sell in the market at a considerable advance: the vain hope of gaining some of the great prizes is the cause of this demand. In order to have a better chance for some of the large prizes, some people purchase several tickets, and others small shares in a still greater number. There is not, however, a more certain proposition in mathematics, than that the more tickets you adventure upon, the more likely you are to be a loser. Adventure upon all the tickets in the lottery and you lose for certain; and the greater the number of your tickets, the nearer you approach to this certainty.

The above is surely a just account of the nature and principles of a Lottery; yet it does not destroy the fact, that, distributed as the tickets always are among thousands, there must be some gainers, and that, in spite of mathematics, there is a lucky number, which must draw the capital prize in the Plymouth Beach Lottery (without any deduction) of 12000 dollars. Both the Historical Dictionary and Lottery Tickets may be had at Cushing and Appleton's old stand, one door west of Central Building;—where BANK BILLS are exchanged.

Lottery at the celebrated "Wayside Inn" at Sudbury in 1760.

THE Managers of Sudbury Lottery, No. Two, hereby notify the Public, That they shall commence Drawing said Lottery, on Friday the Thirtieth Day of May Instant, at the House of Mr. William Bryant Inholder in said Sudbury. ☞ A few Tickets are yet to be had of the Managers, and Samuel Hardcastle and the Printers hereof.

Boston Gazette, May, 1760.

Some remarks in reference to supplying Bibles in the eastern part of Massachusetts by means of a lottery.

MR. RUSSELL,

A FRIEND to religion, and one who wishes the memorial of a certain respectable society may have a happy effect, but a zealous enemy to lotteries, asked a member of an important body, the other day, whether he thought the General Court would grant a Lottery for the purpose of supplying every person in the eastern part of the Commonwealth with a bible, who is unable to purchase one, and for the pay of a missionary.—Let not the serious reader frown, as that member did; for if there is nothing contained in that sacred book which can be thought opposed to this method of gambling, neither the one nor the other can give a substantial reason why, in the present rage for lotteries, the people should not be indulged in raising money in the way most agreeable to their humour.

PERSOLUS.

Columbian Centinel, Feb. 26, 1791.

MRS. CLARK AFLOAT.

In the Ship Ann Maria arrived at New-Haven the following wax passengers, viz. King George III, Bonaparte, Washington, Jefferson, Hamilton, Burr,

Hillhouse, Madison, Pickering, Giles and Mrs. Mary Ann Clark. The Custom-House officers made prisoners of all these passengers for violating the Non-Importation Act, but being proved that they were of East-Haven manufacture and unconscious of crime, we are happy to hear they have been all liberated. King George III. was taken in such bad company as is a sufficient proof that he is crazy. Napoleon undoubtedly rejoiced when he beheld the faithful execution in our waters, of his continental system. Washington and Hamilton were glad that they were in their graves, before their country had been plunged so deeply in disgrace. Had not Pickering and Hillhouse been indeed made of wax, they would have thrown Bonaparte and Jefferson overboard and given them the freedom of the Seas. If the custom-house officers had kept possession of Poor Madison, they could never have obtained much money for him, as he now is a sorry figure, since he has been scalped and tomahawked by Smith. Burr, the democratic vice-president and traitor, who has now gone home to France, ought to be exhibited for the instruction of the People, in every village. Giles must have been liable to have been York-sheared by Mrs. Clark, who, on a July day, when the weather was at blood heat, must have been in a melting mood and susceptible of impressions. But he is an advocate of Non-Intercourse. The officers of the Revenue, notwithstanding they were in such a taking fit, and had conceived such vain and high blown hope of the immense wealth they should receive as the ransom of their Captives, have not half so good a chance of a prize as those adventurers who will call at Cushing and Appleton's, one door west of central Building, and purchase a Ticket or quarter in Harvard College Lottery now drawing.
Salem Gazette, July 12, 1811.
Mr. Pardon Sheldon, a respectable citizen of Providence, was the fortunate holder of the $20,000 prize in the North Carolina Lottery which was drawn some days since.
Salem Observer, Dec. 17, 1825.
A Speedy Cure for a Broken Fortune.
TO all those who bitterly complain of the great dearth of "the root of all evil," and a want of confidence in these speculating times, and who, tremblingly anticipate a long and doubtful conflict, in money operations the coming season, the following beautiful and brilliant schemes offer the means of a sure and an immediate relief.
The Grand State Lottery, Fourth Class Extra, with a capital prize of $10,000, a prize of 500, and 5 prizes of 1000, will draw THIS DAY. Tickets $3 and parts in proportion.
The Rhode-Island Lottery, First Class, New Series, highest prize 10,000, five prizes of 1,000, and a variety of smaller prizes, will draw on the 24th inst. Tickets $3 and parts in proportion. And last, though not least,
The New-York Literature Lottery, Class No. 3, for 1825, with the truly

splendid prizes of 100,000, 50,000, and 10,500 and smaller prizes to the amount of more than half a MILLION of DOLLARS, will draw on the 4th of January next. Tickets $50, and parts in proportion.

For Prizes in the above Lotteries apply to

E.H. PAYSON,

At Dana and Fenno's Office, Central street.

Official Lists of the two first Lotteries will be received by E.H.P. on the evenings of the days of the drawings.   tf   Dec 10.

Salem Observer, 1825.

Fortune's Favourite Sons,

ARE informed that Stonington Point Meeting-House Lottery will positively commence drawing the 19th of May—viz. this day four weeks. In this Lottery of only 6000 Tickets, are one of 3000 dollars—one of 1000—five of 500—two of 400—three of 300—ten of 200—twenty of 100, andc. Tickets for 3 Dollars, for sale, and prizes in the Eastern Stage Road Lottery, taken in pay.—Also Cash paid for those sold by Thomas Hildrup.

N.B. Adventurers may know their fate from his List of Prizes.

Hartford, April 21, 1794.

Connecticut Courant.

To show how largely men's minds—and perhaps women's too—were filled with the lottery mania, if we may so call it, in the days of which we are writing, we will introduce a Southern scheme from the "Petersburg Intelligencer" of 1816, copied in the "Salem Register," September 11 of that year. Some of our readers may think that it is not a bad idea.

From the Petersburg Intelligencer.

MATRIMONIAL LOTTERY

On the 21st day of December last, I was passing through the state of South Carolina, and in the evening arrived in the suburbs of the town of ——, where I had an acquaintance, on whom I called. I was quickly informed that the family was invited to a wedding at a neighboring house, and on being requested, I changed my clothes and went with them. As soon as the young couple were married, the company was seated, and a profound silence ensued—(the man of the house was religious.) A young Lawyer then arose, and addressed the company very handsomely, and in finishing his discourse begged leave to offer a new scheme of matrimony, which he believed and hoped would be beneficial. And obtaining leave he proposed:

That one man in the company should be selected as president; that this president should be duly sworn to keep entirely secret all the communications that should be forwarded to him in his official department that night: and each unmarried gentleman and lady should write his or her name on a piece of paper, and under it place the person's name whom they wished to marry; then hand it to the president for inspection, and if any gentleman and lady had reciprocally chosen each other, the president was to inform each of the result; and those who had not been reciprocal in their choices, should have their choice kept entirely secret.

After the appointment of the president, the communications were accordingly handed up to the chair, and it was found that twelve young gentlemen and ladies had made reciprocal choices; but whom they had chosen remained a secret to all but themselves and the president.—The conversation changed and the company respectively retired.

Now hear the conclusion. I was passing through the same place on the 14th of March following, and was informed that eleven of the twelve matches had been solemnized, and that the young gentlemen of eight couples of the eleven had declared that their diffidence was so great that they certainly should not have addressed their respective wives, if the above scheme had not been introduced.—☞ Gentlemen under 20 and ladies under 15 were excluded as unmarriageable.

You will be pleased to let the public hear of this scheme, and I hope it will be productive of much good, by being practised in Virginia.

A Married Man without Children.

The weak spot in this plan, we imagine, would be the difficulty in keeping the blanks entirely secret.

We have not undertaken to give an account of all the lotteries of which we have seen advertisements, as our limits would not admit of it, even if it could be made interesting to those who like to read about such matters; New England alone would fill a large volume. We will name only a few of the more prominent lotteries,—the Land Bank, in 1759; the Pavement on Boston Neck, the same year. Then there was the Charlestown lottery, the Hatfield Bridge, Sudbury, the Amoskeag Canal, the South Hadley Canal, the Philanthropic, the Kennebec, the Dartmouth College, the Gloucester Road, the Plymouth Beach, etc. All these, of course, were public lotteries, and were managed by the first men in the community. In relation to private lotteries it would now be difficult to ascertain the facts. There must have been a great number of these; probably they were not always honestly conducted. We have heard that there were shops where the inexperienced were supplied with bogus tickets,—blanks of some drawn lottery. Bad men, unfortunately, are to be found in all kinds of business; but we know that in Salem all the men whose names we have mentioned were among the very best in the community.

Although laws are now in force in Massachusetts and some other States against lotteries, there appears to be no essential difference, as far as the morality of the thing is concerned, between the old lottery and the modern raffle,—and indeed a certain species of stock gambling, it seems to us, is worse than either in its moral effects. After the year 1826, or thereabout, lotteries appear to have become unpopular, and laws were passed prohibiting them. Their unprofitableness, moreover, seems then to have been more clearly seen. As we have already said, there had always been some who saw the evils which must result from such schemes. Notably among prominent men who in Massachusetts used their influence against them were John Hancock,[1] of Revolutionary fame, and afterwards governor of the Commonwealth, and Peter C. Brooks, a distinguished merchant of Boston, father-in-law of Edward Everett. The "Salem Gazette" of Sept. 16, 1794, says: "Considering the acknowledged immoral tendency of Lotteries, it is astonishing how much is said in the Boston papers in favor of that which our Legislature has lately instituted for Harvard College. Our late worthy Governor Hancock, in a public address to the General

Court, gave his testimony against this species of gambling, so calculated to ensnare and injure those classes of worthy citizens who are guiltless of that vice in its common form."

[1] Although we have seen lottery tickets signed by Hancock earlier in life.

In some foreign countries and in a few of the States of our Union lotteries are still lawful; yet we believe there is a growing feeling against them. But if stock gambling is destined to take the place of the lottery, we do not think much will be gained by the change. The losses by lotteries were generally in small sums, and could be better borne by the adventurers than the entire loss of property, health, and reputation which is now too apt to follow a large proportion of the speculative stock operations. In the lottery, too, the risks were generally so small that the ticket-buyer alone suffered; whereas now, whole families are often involved in financial ruin, if not in disgrace, by the operations of a father, brother, or near relative. But we will say no more on this point, as it is a consideration foreign to the object of this book.

Thus far we have written mainly of American lotteries; as it is not our intention to take an exhaustive view of the subject, we will merely say, in reference to foreign countries, that lotteries were instituted in England in 1567, and abolished by Act of Parliament in 1823, although allowed until 1826, when the last drawing of a legal lottery took place. During this period they were patronized by all classes,—royalty, the nobility, gentry, and commoners. The first lottery was for the repairs of harbors and fortifications. The drawing took place at the "west door of St. Paul's Church." In 1612 King James I. granted a lottery for the "English Colonies in Virginia, ... to be held at the west end of St. Paul's," and "one Thomas Sharplys, a tailor, drew the chief Prize, which was 4000 crowns in fair plate."

To this day the lottery flourishes in most of the chief cities in Europe, and lottery tickets are vended in many shops as well as in regular offices. The Cologne Cathedral, as is well known, was only recently finished by the aid of a lottery. Lotteries are upheld, we believe, by the Roman Catholic Church in Europe, and many of the priests aid in disposing of the tickets,— at least so we have been told.

The sum of the whole matter as regards this country is that a good work was undoubtedly accomplished through the agency of the lottery in the early days of our national history. By its aid schools, colleges, and charities were founded, bridges, roads, and canals were constructed. In our time public opinion is, of course, as it ought to be, against gambling in any form; but although our ways are almost always thought to be more honest, it is a question, after all, whether we are really more upright than our fathers, who sometimes engaged in transactions that are condemned by modern society, but who, on the other hand, knew nothing of "defaulted" railroad bonds, of

"wild cat" oil companies, or of "watered" mining stocks. It is easy enough to
"Compound for sins [we] are inclined to,
By damning those [we] have no mind to."

www.ingramcontent.com/pod-product-compliance
Lightning Source LLC
Chambersburg PA
CBHW071133280526
45787CB00003B/1269